Roman

is a

BIGGER

Brother

DJ Stutz

illustrated by Nadiia Kolpak

Roman is a BIGGER Brother

This is a work of fiction.

Printed in the United States of America

A 2 Z Press LLC

3670 Woodbridge Rd

Deland, FL 32720

bestlittleonlinebookstore.com

sizemore3630@aol.com

440-241-3126

ISBN: 978-1-962101-13-4

Dedication:

*To Roman and Niko -
two brothers who get it*

This book belongs to

_____

This is Roman and
his dog Harley.
Roman lives with his mom and
dad and life is pretty good.

One day Roman's parents sat down with him and said, "We have some very exciting news. You are going to be a big brother soon." "Hooray!" said Roman. And Roman felt **EXCITED**, but he wasn't quite sure why.

That night, as Mom and Dad tucked him into bed and gave him kisses, Roman asked, "If we have a new baby, will you love it more than me?"

Mom and Dad smiled and gave him an extra hug. "The funny thing about love is that it can grow and grow. In your life you will love many people; all at the same time," said Dad.

Mom smiled and told him, "We will always love you. No matter how many children come to our family, you will always be our Roman." And Roman felt **LOVED**.

The next day Roman was playing with his friend Maylee. She had a baby in her family, so Roman asked her what it was like. Maylee told him, "Oh, it is fun. The baby is so cute, and she smells so good. And when she wraps her little hand around your finger your heart just sings. When she laughs it is like magic and I have to laugh with her every time."

"Hmmm," thought Roman, "that doesn't sound so bad." And Roman felt **HOPEFUL**.

Then Roman talked with his friend Zane. "Uck!" exclaimed Zane. "Babies are horrible! They stink and they cry, and they puke and they take all of Mom's time! She has to feed the baby, and hold the baby, and wash the baby. It never stops! Then your dad is always taking care of the baby so you mom can sleep. They aren't even fun to play with. They can't talk, they can't build anything, and they don't even know how to throw a ball. Babies are awful!"

"Oh, no," Roman worried. "Maybe this isn't going to be so good after all," and Roman felt **CONFUSED**.

After school, Roman decided to just hang out in his tree house in the back yard. He had so many feelings. He was **NERVOUS** about this baby coming. He was **CURIOUS** if it was going to be horrible or fun. Was this baby going to be disgusting or cute?

Was Mom still going to read stories and make snacks? Was Dad still going to play soccer and ride bikes? What about tickle wars? Roman was **CONCERNED**. "Oh Harley," he said, "I know you will always be my friend."

One day, Roman woke up and Mom and Dad weren't there.
His Grandma was in the kitchen cooking his favorite pancakes.
She had a big smile on her face.
"Where's Mom and Dad?" Roman inquired.
"Well," beamed Grandma, "They are at the hospital. Your baby brother is coming today."

Roman's tummy felt funny. He was **EXCITED** to meet his new brother, but he felt a little **NERVOUS** too. Was mommy going to be okay? He heard that it hurts to have a baby. And Roman felt **ANXIOUS**.

When Roman came home from school, Grandma told him to change his clothes and wash his face. They were going to the hospital to meet his new brother. Roman **WONDERED**, 'Was he going to be stinky or would he smell good? Was he going to be crying or laughing?'

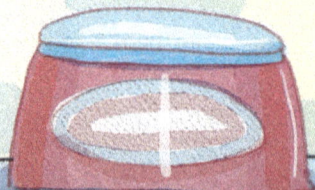

As they walked into the hospital room, Roman saw his Mom and Dad. Mom was in a bed, and she looked happy but tired. Roman ran to her and gave her a big hug. "Are you okay?" he asked. "Did it hurt?" Mom smiled and said, "Yes, it hurt some, but mamas are willing to hurt a little for their children. Would you like to meet your brother? His name is Niko." Roman looked at his dad who was holding Niko. As Roman walked over he felt a little **NERVOUS** and **EXCITED** at the same time. His dad smiled and moved a little so Roman could get a better look.

Niko was so small. He had green eyes and
his lips looked like he was ready to kiss someone.
Dad told him to bring a finger near Niko's tiny hands
and showed him how to be gentle. As Roman put his
finger right by Niko's hand, Niko wrapped his little
fingers around Roman's bigger one.

Roman's heart filled up with a special feeling.
It was like his chest was all warm and peaceful,
and Roman felt so good inside.
"How does that feel?" asked Dad.
"Good," replied Roman.

Actually, it felt **BIGGER** than good, but Roman
couldn't find the right word. He wanted to
feel like this forever. It was a very special
feeling. Maybe his friend Maylee was right!

Mom brought Niko home. It seemed like she was extra busy taking care of Niko, but Mom read stories while she fed Niko and sang songs while she would rock him.

Roman liked that. But sometimes he had to be extra quiet when he was playing because Niko was sleeping. And Roman was **ANNOYED**.

Sometimes Dad played soccer in the yard while Niko was taking a nap. Roman loved their time together and was **HAPPY.**

Occasionally, Niko would cry in the middle of the night while Roman was trying to sleep. He could hear his mom and dad walking around and trying to help Niko.

Usually he stopped crying quickly, but other times he cried for a long time. That made it hard to sleep and Roman felt **EXHAUSTED**.

One afternoon, Roman was playing with his cars and he smelled something and it was NOT good. He looked around the room and he saw Harley. Did Harley toot? He walked over to check, and that smell did not come from Harley and it was getting worse! Then he looked at Niko.
"Mom!" Roman called. "Something smells really bad! I think something is wrong with Niko because it is coming from him."

Mom came into the room. "Oh my goodness," she said. "Niko pooped. We need to change his diaper."
"Holy smokes!" replied Roman. "That smell is poop? That is so disgusting! And what do you mean *we* need to change his diaper?" Roman felt **UNSURE** about this.

On another day, Dad asked Roman to hold Niko while he was fixing some breakfast. Roman decided to make funny faces and noises. Niko seemed to like that. As Roman went to give Niko a big hug he heard something. Something that couldn't be good. As he looked down, he saw a wet white spot on his shirt and on Niko's mouth.

"Ugh!" Roman bellowed. "Dad! He just threw up on me!!"
It smelled bad and felt disgusting.
Dad laughed and took Niko. "Sometimes babies will throw up when they laugh too much. Sometimes they just throw up. You used to throw up on me too," he chuckled.
"It is just part of being a baby."
But Roman felt **NAUSIATED**.

As time went by, Niko grew bigger. One time, Roman and Harley were sitting next to Niko while Mom was doing the dishes. Suddenly, Harley gave a little bark as he saw a squirrel in the tree by the window. Niko looked at Harley and started laughing. Roman smiled and he made a barking sound and Niko laughed again. Roman barked again and again, and Niko laughed so hard. And Roman felt **ECSTATIC**.

Roman was getting used to this big brother thing. Everyone has their own fun parts and difficult parts. Let's face it, even Roman tooted and burped sometimes.

Sometimes, Niko would try to grab Roman's toys. Roman had to be careful to put things away because Niko would put them in his mouth and might choke, not to mention get slobber all over them. That could be so **FRUSTRATING**.

Once, Roman was playing with his cars. One of the wheels on his favorite car wouldn't turn. He became **EXASPARATED** and threw his car across the room. Niko watched him quietly. Then he grabbed another car and threw it as well.

Roman watched him and thought for a minute. Then Roman picked up another car and threw it across the room. He watched as Niko picked up another car and threw it. "Hmmm," Roman thought.
"This is **INTERESTING**."

CLaP
CLaP
CLaP

As time went by, he noticed that Niko often would copy him. If Roman clapped his hands, sometimes Niko would clap his hands. If Roman made a funny noise, Niko would try to make the same noise.
Mom said that being a big brother is a magical thing. Niko would learn so many things from him.

If Roman made good choices, was patient, kind and loving, Niko would be watching and learning. Roman would be the one to choose if they were going to be great friends or argue and be mean. "You can be his hero, or his adversary. And the truth is that there will be times when you get along and times when you don't. That is all part of growing up. But, Roman, no matter what, it will be your job to make sure Niko knows you love him.
All the time."

Roman thought about this and he looked at Niko. Niko looked up and smiled. Roman knew his friends Maylee and Zane were both right. Little brothers are amazing and disgusting and Roman was so glad to be a big brother.

DJ Stutz is an Early Childhood Specialist and understands the importance of vocabulary for a child's success in academics, as well as emotional regulation and developing friendships. She is Mom to 5, Neina to 12 and Auntie to 70. Now, she lives on a farm on a prairie not far from Old Faithful where she coaches parents of young children and works on her podcast, Imperfect Heroes: Insights into Parenting.

Lesson Plan: Exploring Family Emotions
with *Roman is a BIGGER Brother*

Objective: The objective of the lesson plan is to help children ages 4-8 expand their emotional vocabulary by exploring family and sibling relationships. Using *Roman is a Bigger Brother*, children will identify, describe, and understand emotions such as excitement, jealousy, pride, and frustration, along with their synonyms.

Materials Needed:

    The book, "Roman is a BIGGER Brother"
    Whiteboard or large paper for brainstorming
    Flashcards or index cards with family-related emotion words or emojis
    Paper and crayons or colored markers
    Index cards or flashcards
    Small notebook or journal (for older children)

Duration of lesson: Approximately 45 minutes to 1 hour

Introduction Guess and Predict (5 minutes):

    Gather the children in a comfortable reading area and introduce the book "Roman is a BIGGER Brother"

    Show them the cover and ask them what they think the story might be about based on the title and the image on the cover.

    Ask Questions:

        "What do you think the story is about?"
        "Do you think Roman will be excited or unhappy about
            getting a new brother?"
        "Will the new brother be fun or annoying?"
        "Is being a big brother different from being a little brother?"

Encourage Predictions: Invite the children to share their thoughts and guesses about what might happen in the story.

Activities for Ages 4-6

1. **Role Play: Sibling Emotions (10 minutes)**
   Provide flashcards with emojis representing emotions (e.g., happy,
         sad, jealous, proud).
   Have each child pick a card, act out the emotion,
         and let the group guess what it is.
   Discuss when they might feel that way about a sibling.
2. **Story Reactions (10 minutes)**
   After reading the book, ask simple questions like:
   "How do you think Roman felt when his brother was born?"
3. **Drawing Feelings (10 minutes)**

   Ask children to draw a picture of a time they felt happy, jealous, or proud
   about something in their family.

   Label the emotions in the picture and talk about what happened.

Activities for Ages 6-8

1. **Emotion Word Matching (10 minutes)**
   Create flashcards with emotion words from the story
   (e.g., *proud, jealous, frustrated*).
   On separate cards, write synonyms (e.g., *happy, thrilled, annoyed*).
   Have children match the original words with their synonyms and discuss
   how they might use them in sentences.
2. **Writing Prompts (10 minutes)**
   Provide prompts like:
   "Write about a time you felt proud of your sibling."
   "What's something you like to do with your brother or sister?"
   Encourage them to use at least two synonyms for each emotion
3. **Create a Mini-Story (15 minutes)**
   Ask children to write or draw a short story about Roman and his brother.
   Challenge them to include different emotions Roman might
         feel and use synonyms to describe them.

Conclusion: Reflect and Share (5 minutes)

   Group Review: Discuss the emotions Roman felt in the story and the ones
            they explored during activities.
   Encourage Use: Challenge children to use their new words
            when talking about family experiences.
   Praise Participation: Highlight their creativity and thoughtful insights
            about emotions and family.

Note: This lesson plan ensures developmentally appropriate activities for different age groups,
helping all children engage with the material in a meaningful and enjoyable way.

Parent Activity Page: Building Strong Sibling Relationships

Sibling relationships can be full of love, laughter, and learning—but they can also come with challenges. Here are activities to help your children identify emotions common in sibling relationships and learn how to strengthen those bonds through kindness, support, and setting a good example.

Activity 1: Emotion Charades

Purpose: Teach children to recognize and label emotions they might feel toward their siblings.

What You'll Need:
Emotion flashcards or a list of emotions (e.g., happy, jealous, frustrated, proud).

How to Play:
1. Take turns acting out emotions related to sibling interactions, like jealousy over a toy or pride in a sibling's accomplishment.
2. After guessing the emotion, discuss when they've felt that way about their sibling and how they handled it.

Encourage brainstorming ways to respond positively to each emotion.

Activity 2: The Kindness Jar

Purpose: Encourage acts of kindness between siblings.

What You'll Need:
A jar, slips of paper, and a pen.

How to Play:
1. Write down simple acts of kindness on slips of paper (e.g., "Share your favorite toy," "Say something nice about your sibling," "Help them with a chore").
2. Have each child draw a slip daily and complete the act of kindness.
3. Celebrate their efforts at the end of the week with a small reward or family fun time.

Activity 3: Sibling Superpowers

Purpose: Help children appreciate each sibling's unique strengths.

What You'll Need:
Paper and crayons or markers.

How to Play:
1. Ask each child to draw or write about their sibling's "superpowers" (e.g., being funny, good at sports, helpful).
2. Share these with the family and discuss how these strengths make their sibling special.
3. Encourage children to cheer each other on when they see these "superpowers" I   n action.

Teaches Life Skills: Children practice empathy, patience, and teamwork.

By modeling these behaviors and encouraging these activities, you're helping your children build lifelong skills and nurturing a loving sibling relationship.

Activity 4: Problem-Solving Practice
Purpose: Teach conflict resolution skills.

What You'll Need:
A comfortable space for discussion.

How to Play:
1. Role-play common sibling conflicts (e.g., fighting over toys or who gets to go first).
2. Guide children through steps to solve the problem:
   Take turns explaining how they feel.
   Brainstorm solutions together.
   Choose a solution that works for everyone.
   Praise their teamwork and willingness to listen.

Activity 5: Family Kindness Tree

Purpose: Visualize how kind actions grow strong sibling relationships.

What You'll Need:
Large paper, markers, and sticky notes.

How to Play:
1. Draw a tree with branches labeled "Kindness," "Support," and "Being a Good Example."
2. Each time a child does something positive for their sibling, write it on a sticky note and add it as a "leaf" to the tree.
3. Watch the tree grow over time and celebrate the family's kindness!

Activity 6: Sibling Gratitude Letters

Purpose: Foster appreciation between siblings.

What You'll Need:
Paper and pencils.

How to Play:
1. Ask each child to write (or dictate) a short letter to their sibling, thanking them for something they've done or sharing what they love about them.
2. Read the letters aloud as a family to reinforce positive feelings.

Activity 7: Sibling Goals Chart

Purpose: Encourage teamwork and shared goals.

What You'll Need:

A chart or poster board.

How to Play:
1. Set a goal siblings can achieve together (e.g., keeping their playroom clean, playing nicely for a set time).
2. Track their progress on the chart and reward them when they reach the goal.

Benefits of Being Kind, Supportive, and a Good Example

- **Builds Trust:** Siblings learn they can rely on each other.

- **Reduces Conflict:** Kindness and support help prevent fights.

- **Strengthens Bonds:** Positive actions create lasting memories.

- **Teaches Life Skills:** Children practice empathy, patience, and teamwork.

By modeling these behaviors and encouraging these activities, you're helping your children build lifelong skills and nurturing a loving sibling relationship.

A Note from the Author

Dear Readers,

Thank you for joining Roman on his adventures as he navigates the joys and challenges of being a big brother. In this second book, we continue to explore Roman's journey of identifying and understanding his emotions as he grows into his new role in the family. It's a heartwarming tale of love, patience, and the beginning of a beautiful sibling relationship. Keep an eye out for future adventures as Roman and Niko grow together, learning the value of building a strong bond and cherishing their unique connection.

I'd love for you to become part of the conversation! Tune in to the *Imperfect Heroes: Insights into Parenting* podcast, where we share candid discussions, expert interviews, and touching stories that resonate with parents from all walks of life. Access the latest episodes and explore a wealth of parenting insights by visiting our podcast website at www.ImperfectHeroesPodcast.com.

For a more visual experience, check out the podcast episodes as videos on my YouTube Channel https://www.youtube.com/@imperfectheroes/videos or my Rumble Channel https://rumble.com/search/all?q=Imperfect%20Heroes.

Discover more about my parent coaching services and additional resources at www.ImperfectHeroes.net.

Let's connect and keep the conversation going! Join me on social media:

Facebook: The Imperfect Heroes

Instagram: @imperfect_heroes

Thank you for supporting Roman's journey, and I look forward to sharing more stories with you in the future!

Warm regards,

DJ Stutz

www.ingramcontent.com/pod-product-compliance
Lightning Source LLC
Chambersburg PA
CBHW042333030426
42335CB00027B/3329